Life as a Frog

Vic Parker

Heinemann
LIBRARY

Little Nippers

H **www.heinemann.co.uk/library**
Visit our website to find out more information about **Heinemann Library** books.

To order:
☎ Phone 44 (0) 1865 888066
🖨 Send a fax to 44 (0) 1865 314091
💻 Visit the Heinemann Bookshop at www.heinemann.co.uk/library to browse our catalogue and order online.

First published in Great Britain by Heinemann Library, Halley Court, Jordan Hill, Oxford OX2 8EJ, part of Harcourt Education. Heinemann is a registered trademark of Harcourt Education Ltd.

Editorial: Jilly Attwood and Claire Throp
Design: Jo Hinton-Malivoire and bigtop, Bicester, UK
Models made by: Jo Brooker
Picture Research: Catherine Bevan
Production: Séverine Ribierre

Originated by Dot Gradations
Printed and bound in China by South China Printing Company

ISBN 0431 17100 9 (hardback)
07 06 05 04 03
10 9 8 7 6 5 4 3 2 1

ISBN 0431 17105 X (paperback)
07 06 05 04 03
10 9 8 7 6 5 /02 4 3 2 1

British Library Cataloguing in Publication Data
Parker, Vic
Life as a frog
597.8'9
A full catalogue record for this book is available from the British Library.

Acknowledgements
The publishers would like to thank the following for permission to reproduce photographs:
Andy Purcell p. **15**; Bruce Coleman pp. **4-5** (Jane Burton), **22-23** (Feliz Labhardt); FLPA (© W Meinderts) Foto Natur p. **6**; Heather Angel p. **7**; NHPA pp. **8**, **9** (© G I Bernard), **10-11**, **12**, **14** (Stephen Dalton); Oxford Scientific Films p. **16-17**; OSF pp. **13** (© Paul Franklin); OSF p. **20-21** (Ian West); Woodfall Wild Images p. **18-19**.

Cover photograph reproduced with permission of Naturepl.com/William Osborn

The publishers would like to thank Annie Davy for her assistance in the preparation of this book.

Every effort has been made to contact copyright holders of any material reproduced in this book. Any omissions will be rectified in subsequent printings if notice is given to the publishers.

Contents

What can you see in the pond water?

Lots of dots in wibbly wobbly jelly.

It is called frogspawn.

Tiny tadpoles

The dots are eggs. The frogspawn hatches into tiny tadpoles.

Wiggle!

A tadpole has a long wiggly tail.

Making changes

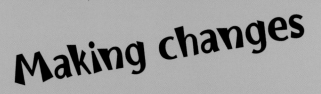

After six weeks the tadpole
starts to grow legs.

The tadpole's legs grow longer and its tail grows shorter.

Slowly, the tadpole turns into ...

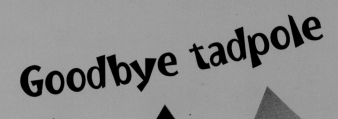

Goodbye tadpole

... A frog!

Life in water

The frog lives in ponds and rivers.

Plop!

It is an excellent
swimmer.

Life on land

The frog can live on land, too.

HOP!

It likes damp, dark places.

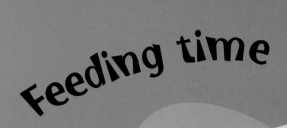

A worm is a tasty treat for the frog.

It is gone in one gulp!

Meeting a mate

Sometimes a male frog calls a female frog to come to meet him.

Laying eggs

The female frog
lays frogspawn.

The frogspawn will
turn into tadpoles.
The tadpoles will soon
become...

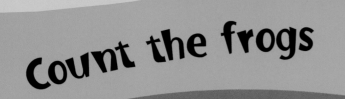
Count the frogs

... Lots of new frogs!

Index

The end

Notes for adults

The **Life as a** . . . series looks at the life cycles of familiar animals and plants, introducing the young child to the concept of change over time. There are four titles in the series and when used together, they will enable comparison of similarities and differences between life cycles. The key curriculum early learning goals relevant to this series are:

Knowledge and understanding of the world
- find out about, and identify, some features of living things that the young child observes
- ask questions about why things happen
- differentiate between past and present.

This book takes the reader on a circular journey from the beginning of a frog's life as frogspawn, through its developmental stages (including habitat and what the tadpole needs to grow), to maturity and reproduction. The book will help children extend their vocabulary, as they will hear new words such as *frogspawn* and *tadpole*. You might like to introduce the word *webbed* when looking at the frog's feet. It may be helpful to explain to young readers that many of the photographs are larger than life size.

Additional information about frogs

Frogs are amphibians – a group of creatures which are vertebrates, carnivorous, and able to live both in water and on land. Toads, newts and salamanders are all amphibians. Amphibians have existed on Earth for millions of years and are found in every continent except Antarctica. Toads generally have drier, wartier skin than frogs, and have shorter hind legs which are better for walking than jumping. There are more than 3,700 species of frogs and toads. The smallest frog in the world is found in Brazil, measuring 8.5mm. The biggest frog is the goliath from West Africa, which measures up to 80cm when stretched out.

Follow-up activities

- Go pond-dipping in Spring to collect a jar of frogspawn. When the tadpoles have emerged, return it to the pond and revisit at weekly intervals to observe their development into frogs.
- Draw, paint or make a model of a frog.